Star Map

+

Nancy Anne Miller

FUTURECYCLE PRESS

www.futurecycle.org

Library of Congress Control Number: 2015960544

Published by FutureCycle Press
Lexington, Kentucky, USA

ISBN 978-1-938853-39-5

With gratitude for my Farmington CT days, where I first learned to interpret the seasons.

CONTENTS

STAR MAP

BLONDES HAVE MORE FUN

Simply the Fourth

Metaphor Hunting

STAR MAP

Tulips in January

They bend as if color is heavy to bear, the weight
of worth as one stem brought a fortune in 1637 trade.

Still proud of that, even the light's gold can't get them
to open. Heads lowered like snakes uncharmed by music.

Held in a crystal vase the way winter holds us each
in glassy ice, surrounds us with what breaks, cracks,

then sends the softness of snow. Petals open in slow
motion, aspergillums sprinkle the room with a silence.

Undress for death, litter the table with taffeta skirt
panels like crushed love letters or painted nails.

Sepals, electrical plugs without the currency of the sun
coursing through, spent from the charge of the moment.

WHITE LIGHT

Everything is converted as white light
pours out of heaven and trees become
thin-ribbed angels who cannot
lift droopy wings to fly. No need to go
up when a celestial world comes down.

The town truck forms its own flapping,
feathery path to us. The steady snow
fills all distances flown between,
leaves arched branches, discarded
scaffolding of flight no longer needed.

Footprints where messengers landed
with a gravitas now dissolve, fill in,
buttonholes buttoned up as a cloak
covers all of the land, is thrown
down for only God to walk over.

An American Day

I bunch the newspapers for the fire,
crunch them, toss them back from
left to right hand, a baseball pitcher

at base, getting ready to throw.
The flames *crack! crack!* the
sound of a bat making a hit.

The sun will rise shortly on
its home run, the winter trees
lift arthritic fingers up to catch.

MERCY

Something good in the grey,
the dreary in-between, a purgatorial smoke
wafting between the burnt-out death of autumn
and the birth and bright blaze of Christmas.

Everything calmly noticeable
in a low-key way.
Nothing takes the eye to the horizon;
what is near is the focus.

So when white falls
like light from heaven, we want it to,
so hungry for this piece of bread
pushed through the bars of trees.

White Elephants

The dark trunks appear early November,
thrust up to the sky like an elephant
washing body and haunches with water,
as last leaves drift down with a splash.

A hand touches the sky's cool waters
to bless oneself; an anointment is made
before going into winter's cathedral
of quietude and large shifts of light.

Unlike a long-memoried mammoth,
fall is full of forgetfulness when summer
shreds sun-full days right in front of
our eyes. The scaffolding of nature

appears firm, thick in bones. When snow
makes trees swell again, they are
the white tusked beasts of Burma's
princes: immense, dear, about to melt.

Snowfall

I think of what we cannot hold,
claim, although it might lie
down flat and white
as linens folded in a drawer.

Even those boxes of wood
stacked in a bureau become coffins,
the fabric inside fraying
like the tattered skin of a person's body.

Even when we put a mothball in,
small as a moon to prevent darkness
and vacant as an evil eye
for anyone who would try to rob a grave.

Skittish

The faces of the deer,
pointed as flint spearheads,
chip at the snow, winter,
at anything that prevents
their feeding.

Heads full frontal,
soft as valentines,
lick the world
cold as ice cream,
so sweet.

Just like the heart
has to dig, dig
to get what it wants,
must be that hungry,
know when to melt.

CRUEL ENOUGH

that the trees have become wallflowers
against the dim sky, stand in a shirking
beauty, all limbs and chipped bark.

Cruel enough, but snow makes all
white! A blank, no references.
Cruel enough stiff colonial houses:

clouds of incense rise from chimneys,
purge environs; smoke twines into a rope,
an escape to heaven. Cruel enough a publisher

says most poetry books end up as pulp like
the shredded ice now landing everywhere,
but so cruel I have to write this poem about it.

Shadowboxing Winter

Hard to swing at something,
comes in droves, ghosts, here
then not there, a gaslighting.

Hard to hit what moves away
as white extends space around
what is still. Hard to heed

the call to go find the horizon
as snow removes nearness,
loads up each footstep, sinks

one down at the beginning in
holes while land shimmers,
flutters like a wing over there.

It Hints of Madness

It hints of madness, the icicles
drooling from roofs, constant snow
a kind of foaming. Like a moon

it came in too close, crash-landed,
combusted cool white light
everywhere. The starched

colonial houses on the green
lose a Victorian presence, slats with
pleats in heavy cotton, the picket

fence a corset undone or a straight
jacket unable to contain ice
the sky spits into its sharp teeth.

The statue of Mary in front of
the church so dwarfed: the world
has marbled her grief, becomes it.

LATE DECEMBER SNOW

Who doesn't want to be buried
by the end of the year?

A return to dust that is
white, luminous, holy?

To be hidden under nature's
drop cloth, bleached, completely clean?

A gauze that wraps, bandages
all the open sores. The year's

accumulated hurts put on ice.
The landscape is blank as

unfilled calendar days, soothes
the cluttered mind. So sit

by the fire, red as blood,
drawn up from a deep wound.

On Not Writing Another Poem About Snow

Sure, windshield wipers protrude
outward, feelers, make cars
into insects, meet death by
eating too much icing on a cake.

And, yes, scraggly bits of dry
stalks push up, are springs
in a mattress, poke through
the season's long white sleep.

The flicker of snowdrops, gnats
drawn to the embalmed skin
of the landscape, the swollen
icy surface of winter days.

Tire tracks make a vertebrae,
a backbone in the road's
middle, hopefully prevent
my swaying into a bend.

No, I need not write another
poem about translucency so
bright, the world strips itself
down in order to receive it.

Hammock in Winter

The V-shaped steel rod
support for the Hatteras Island
hammock pokes up in

descending snow, crooked
airplane wings, an open beak
of a bird carrying the heavy

weight of winter's message.
Two stick-figure ostriches, bent over,
bury heads. The white, white,

becomes summer's breezy bed,
covers the land. Each drop
a hole in the lacework of *macramé*

roping: captures tree, bush,
branch. Imagine swinging back,
forth, back in August's perpetual

humidity, honeysuckle fragrant
in the air like how the world sways
in the blur of sleet about to erase it.

STAR MAP

The frost on my windshield with
connecting white stellar shapes is
a star map left to guide me. How

horrified I was this morning not to
be able to find Point Finger Road on
my Bermuda map. The needle in

my Saab's compass points north,
shaped like an ancestor's cedar ship
pulled up, not down, on the high seas.

And unlike one lost in the haystack
of wily wintry roads, one path threads
its slit eye, a tongue slips through, speaks.

Rorschach Test

All kinds of greenery tied with red ribbons,
branches festooned with bows like a horse's tail
adorned; the rosettes of wreaths hang everywhere,
harness the woods' offerings into seasonal ritual.

How patchy the landscape gets after
Christmas like Appaloosas and pied ponies,
a mangy distortion of brown puddling white,
the friskiness of nature unbound.

Intermittently, a snowstorm covers raw
bones with the vanity of hiding gawky
elbows, knees. Furniture draped in
a grand summer room off-season.

Except dark lines of trees, estuaries
and tributaries of bark against sky's
blue, map our journey into solace:
the Rorschach tests we dress with meanings.

Winter Landscape

The perfect metaphor for memory,
distilling, abstracting,
simplifying what occurred.

When the truth is the meltdown
of what is underneath,
odd-shaped, patchy, not clean.

We sift things through time:
gentle white lies fall,
sugarcoat what is unseemly.

We remember in bits, fill in
in pieces. Our minds joggle:
a snow globe covers the scene.

Keep all in its bubble container
until we dare to enter the winter
landscape of this piece of paper.

White Wash

The roofs on Bermuda houses are
thickly capped as drifts from
a blizzard that blows through
the Northeast. I paint my studio

floor in Connecticut "latex bianco,"
enjoy the calm luxury of the stroke
like a workman spreading lime
over the roofs of Bermuda homes.

Snow falls outside, blurs up, down.
The same dislocation I feel with
a blank sheet of paper where,
just like "those byes" whitewashing

the limestone shingles peaked at
a precarious angle, in lines going
back and forth across the sky, I will
attempt to purify what falls from heaven.

Blondes Have More Fun

Cornfield Early Spring

All vertebrae and broken bones
pulled out of their sockets
from the weight of death.

Corn stalks matted as
the hair of a corpse,
dry leaves curled like maggots.

Cobs discarded from the cold's
machinery like old radio batteries.
This is where winter got wrecked.

Maple Sugar

From afar the white buckets
look like sugar cubes.

Closer, they evoke a sense
of pails for cow's milk.

How is it something so spare
as trees without foliage

could give a sweetness?
The ones with jugs are thin

as African women nursing
a child during famine. Winter

starves the senses, makes
us willing to rob the dead.

MARCH

This is not a dance,
no display of boughs
bowing, bending to partner
in color ripe for a ball.

Hard-won buds emerge
on branches, brass stars
on a soldier's shoulders.
This is not a gift, wrapped

up, ready to open. Instead
buried maple leaves
are hands digging,
digging to find promise

inside the earth. Instead,
this is a march, everything
in place to move precisely,
nothing out of step.

April Snow

A kind of exercise
in pointillism,
dots everywhere punch
holes in my vision.

In Paris, it was about
color, the eye,
how the iris radiates light
into many coins in a fountain.

Each flake drifts down
in a kind of "spot on" way,
similar to what one sees
before a heart is attacked.

The season sneaks in as
daffodils hold thimbles of
yellow. A teaspoon of honey
to chase away winter's ills.

SALUTE

The maple, oak, elm trunks, branches
are harness straps inside a parachute,
clouds the canopy that flew away.

Piles of dirty snow on the ground
are like pilot chutes bunched after
landing. Pre-spring has ups, downs.

The rhododendron husks of dry seeds,
like fat robins, bend branches until
each blade of grass is a salute to the sky.

IGNITION

The forsythia bushes
with bare curving branches
rope light with lasso twirls.

Bear the first yellow buds,
rotate like a lit firecracker
circling within its own energy.

Nature's battery cables spark
everything, help get it going
after winter's battery goes dead.

Until we hear someone somewhere
start up a lawn mower and
spring's machinery is moving.

INVERSE

The pink, yellow, purple, orange
plastic Easter eggs tied to forsythia

branches look like yo-yos, bounce
up and down at the end of string.

This is the season of resurrections;
everywhere we see the pull

between gravity and flight.
The bunny hops, hops, almost

takes off with ears deflated
balloons—need more air!

This bush, twiggy, cross-hatched,
an inverted basket with jelly

beans on the exterior. Lent is
when the world is inside out.

Confinement

The March landscape has an insect feel,
with stick appendages pokey,
clumped leafless bushes like spiders.

In solitary confinement, prisoners
speak to bugs, name them,
give out crumbs, just for company,

life. Likewise, whatever begins
to fill winter's solitary space,
creeps the horizon, I greet. Eager

for forsythia's curved feelers to
drip bits of yellow, like scythes
which have finally sliced open the sun.

Litter Pick

I want to wield one, as seen used by
people hired in parks to pick up litter.
I want to jab each piece of snow like
unwanted trash to clean up the land.

And the larger mounds, small hills,
swelling, rolling here and there, I
want to harpoon the backs of, the curve
of a great white whale diving. I would

get down on my knees, remove the moist
cloth wrapped around the earth, eager
as a sculptor to touch the rumpled face
of a cast left in the overnight studio.

BLONDES HAVE MORE FUN

Blondes do have more fun. See, already
the willow lets down hair, sweeps
the early March field while other trees
line the sky with a greyness, wait for

a color job. The daffodils cue up,
shout through megaphones, cheerleaders
that they are, blast passersby with news
about coming bright days. Even dandelions

wake up with uncombed mops and get
a free pass into everyone's lawn. Finally
that shooting star, the fast yellow line
streaking the middle of the road

halving winter into going and coming,
has led to where forsythia whips
the stone wall like a donkey, beast
of burden, to get up out of the ditch.

SIMPLY THE FOURTH

Just When

Just when the dark shadows spill
ink on summer's page of light

and I lie in a string hammock,
caught in the web, net of dreams.

The daylilies climb, charmed as
snakes, listen to growing things. Wear

a pronged jester's hat for June, July;
live one day at a time. May I be so

foolishly spent, like flowers twist,
coil by night, rags wrung out from use.

Wrought Iron Bed

The "Estate Sale" sign misleads,
there are only a few pieces of furniture
in the driveway of an old farm.

Wrought iron headboard, footboard
painted white like a stream of milk
flows through machinery while

the hired hands sleep. The steely
outline of angel wings comes to
lift the tired away from daily toil.

Two gates: one keeps a dreamer
penned in, one swings open, leads
cows up to a high green meadow.

Simply the Fourth

A flag a child could draw, so right for such a young country.
No emblems, or crowns, just a bunch of stars to reach for
and the fast lines of movement for roads anyone can find.

The food is simply cooked around a fire from early days.
Meat made grabble in buns, soft in the hand like a catcher's mitt.
Chips break in the mouth, hosts for the moment's celebration.

Likewise, firecrackers shoot above and then fade quickly,
party souvenirs thrown away in the bin. Everyone wears tee
shirts, sandals, baseball caps. Nothing impedes going forth.

The Sky's Graffiti

The daylilies from White Flower
Farm are many colored: yellow,
pink, a tawny red. I deadhead
them. The twisted buds like

plump paint tubes leak color
at the top. The sky's canvas
cannot be filled although the
wild orange ones counterpoint

the blue, try to complement its
hazy shimmer. The sky's canvas
cannot be filled although on
the Fourth we light firecrackers

to write graffiti across it. An
attempt to own the night, like walls
demarked in cities, where scribbles
are fuses lit, spinning in circles, circles.

Not England

New England, Not England in so
many ways, not this obsession
with L.L., a Long Lineage
Bean one hopes to transplant
just by wearing catalogue clothes.
I remember Edwards, our West

Indian gardener, clips hedges
in January in a Harris Tweed.
Rita irons in her cashmere
sweater without much ado.
Bought at Smith's in Hamilton,
where everyone shopped. The regard

for Hitchcock furniture made
without a hitch baffles, no nuanced
bump or truth-telling error, no
wee crack Sir Alfred might find.
And pies put on dinner tables like
doilies to decorate a meal. Yes,

England, the land with curves
and hills verdant, stone walled
into generous fields, but Not
England this array of four full
seasons the terrain changes into,
a mad search for identity and whom to be.

DAYLILY

The day is a lily, a bud
balloons, bursts orange
at the end of a long
green string. The day is a lily,

a bud wrings out hours
of light. A rag in the hand
of a woman washing
down the sky. The day is

a lily with fingers crossed
tight. To wish the sun,
an O, an antiphon will praise
morning into being again.

Sun Gold Tomato

To eat light, the light that makes seeded
earth pop, grow sweetness. Light bulb

-ed on green extension cords, sun
electrifies, moon teaches to be

roundness. Light, we swallow, know
we once were seed too, grew into round

flesh and popped, a pink bud between
the leaves, the curl of our mother's legs.

LIVID

The Queen Anne floats
above the land, clouds
of heat from the July earth.

Wiry as a cooking thermometer,
presses into the flanks of
the hill, registers white hot, livid.

I think of the few queens you are
named after. Boil with resentment,
yet stand straight and tall, lace

collars foaming from an inner fury.
A summer moth pinned down by
a taxidermist's needle tries to fly to the sun.

Summer White

Something so pure
about a morning glory
at the end of summer.

Bleached by the sun,
like any laundered fabric.
A Dixie Cup for water

to soothe in the heat.
A handkerchief to wipe
away the raspberry stain

bleeding from the mouth,
like lipstick worn on
the constant first date summer is.

Raspberries

Clusters of taste buds
lick the summer heat.
Summer's sweetness has
pimpled into berries.

Everything about them
is adolescent and gawky.
Long stems poke out
from the body of leaves.

There is no stamina
to meet a frost. I collect
what is left. Purple goose
bumps shivering in the cold.

AUGUST SPIDER

The daddy longlegs forms a map,
a village center with many roads in.

Hangs on the window screen, a clock;
hour and second hands multiply,

regulate the day. It is the crack
time is, wispy, spindly, creeps into

far corners. Appendages, multi-
threads, try to go through an eye,

break, fray. A pocket watch dangles
on a silk chain, stops a summer moment.

MAZE

Like love it symbolizes,
the rose is a soft, soft maze,
tightens at the center.

Stem's five fingers
push each petal away,
a breezy door into openness.

Veils drop, reveal stamen's
knob. Only memory
can turn to enter.

Ripe

My Saab smells like a ripe cheese
inside, a triple crème at full age.
Yellow tennis balls are from some sort
of fondue. Orange plastic trainer,

a goat milk variety, sprouts
knobby spores. My dog stinks,
like seaweed on the beach, coat
wet days after a swim. It is too soon

for summer to rot, sour. August
claustrophobic, tree trunks,
L.P. record holders spin the season's
green vinyl disk, over, over again.

FIREFLIES

The summer lifeguards have retrieved
the ropes and buoys that marked a safe
swim area. Like the knotted and beaded
string bracelets worn on vacation wrists of
teenagers, time to put them away. I toss

a yellow tennis ball for my Irish Water Spaniel,
a sun he won't let sink below the water.
He goes back, forward to replay the same
scene, prevent a day's end; drops the ball at
my feet so I can make it curve the sky with

brightness. He shakes water off as if he
has broken through glass, a time sphere
into the next season we both embrace. No
need to hoard August days like fireflies in
a jar which in the dark glow like treasure.

Summer's Beggar

It all points to going to the ocean at the end
of the season where wave by wave summer
is covered, buried, taken into the deep. Shells

are scattered at the edge of the tide, loose
change falling out of the rim of a skirt
for me to pick up, summer's beggar. I will

bring a large conch back, itself a whirl,
a turning. Place it on my shelf to stay still,
slow. A snail crawls endlessly through winter.

METAPHOR HUNTING

LET'S NOT PRETEND

Let's not pretend you don't like
the crisp light, the way the wrinkled
leaves rattle in dry color with
ragged edges shafts of winter sun

will iron out. Let's not pretend
you don't like the way the tree
lets go of foliage, like an unclasped
barrette releases strands of flaxen

hair. Let's not pretend you don't
enjoy the first maroon leaf deep
in branches, like the first redbird
sits in April. Let's not pretend you

don't welcome a shower of debris,
like seconds of your life swirl,
descend, so now you can look
up into the eternally deep blue.

Let's not pretend you don't hold
your breath when the orange maple
fingers green with its glove, holding
dearly onto summer, while inside

the stiff trunk circles another year,
carves a steady turn like a coil
tightens into a spring sprung,
makes such a golden sky fall.

Short Circuit

The world has blown a fuse:
trees short circuit, sizzle light.

Vines spark like live wires
wrapped around walls, fences.

A sudden bareness reminds
how full summer is. Absence

displayed on the stiff hanger
of branches, a silky see-through slip.

I am exposed. Exhausted too.
Can't step out of clothes. I drop,

still as the trunk in the circle
of leaves seeping into roots

and, unlike the carved ring inside,
not whirling, expanding, opening.

Autumn Sounds

The leaves on the ground
crackle as rain hits hard,
like popcorn roasts or
Kellog's Rice Krispies crunch
when morning milk is poured.

The trees pop a burnt color
in the sky's microwave,
when in an instant foliage
fries and the lawn is a rug
full of discarded, crumbly crisps.

With the buoyancy of a trapeze,
the ground gives with a bounce,
could send you skyward as
everything falls down, propels
you up, just from the light of it.

Autumn

Leaves are monarch butterflies,
curl back into the brown
crawl of caterpillars. An album's

tattered pages crumble across
my backyard. I let what should
die in me die. I rake,

heap up dry brittle piles,
moths that have fallen off
the lamp of the sun.

Landscape as Painting

The ruination is Rembrandt,
the chipped paint from a masterpiece,
the exquisite glory of death
going out gold, ripe in beauty.

Soon November will be muddy,
streaked with ordinary brown:
Soutine's hungry brushstrokes,
trees picked clean as the bones of a chicken.

I will begin to fast then too
as winter's clean plate,
abstract as Malevich's canvas,
fills space while emptying it.

STARRY SKY

Today the landscape is very Van Gogh:
the black lines of trees, flecks of gold
everywhere; a starry sky drips. Trees

bend like crows scavenging, burst
from too much color: a mind with
too much light. Think of a scarecrow

in the field, unable to keep the dark
away. Think of hurried paint strokes
as seed the wind scatters and sows.

Summer's Widow

Dressed to kill, the maple is full of gold,
red, yellow. If you are going to die,
be beautiful in the moment. Let wind
lift you in a last dance that reveals
the curvaceous reach of your branches.

If you age, age well, and cause envy
from the audience. Before you drop,
surprise everyone with your complexity.
Don't go quietly out but howl with
a presence before letting go.

And if that isn't enough, just reappear!
A ghost rising up the long thin trunk
of a chimney's neck with smoke
unfurling and spreading leaves,
reaching across the entire sky.

MOCCASIN

Indian summer
turns the yard
into patches
of brown and grey,
an Appaloosa's flank.

Bright yellow leaf,
a feather
from a squaw
passing.

The woods
all hushed and quiet,
a season moves
in moccasins.

Trees light presences
here, then gone,
leave the sun's ring exposed,
a campfire still smoking.

CHANGE

The first leaves have turned
here in the hollow
at the bottom of a low branch.

These bright patches
are coins in a deep pocket
waiting to be spent.

The first tithes
for the season ahead
of constant change.

An early bet placed
with a handful of money
to win a toppling sum
of gold piled to the sky.

In Hock

Leaves cover the ground.
I have enough pawn tickets
to get the sun out of hock
every winter night;
every winter night cold surrounds it.

It reappears each a.m. in
the thinned hand of the bare tree,
a magician's trick
to make a coin
come out of the blue.

I can't believe it is there
until warm fingers
touch my back, arms and legs,
planted down in spring's soft earth
with the spindly roots of shadow.

Falling

A hard time to fall in love,
what with the landscape
letting go, letting go, releasing.
Nothing is permanent. Leaves

are everywhere, hands cut
off from holding onto, trying to
steal too much sky. The sun
litters too, throwing parts

of itself away; pieces of it
still shine everywhere. Is
this love's work? To be made
naked, vulnerable, stripped

to the core? I stand like a tree
amongst debris, a passenger
who has discarded all tickets
to any other destination.

Iffy

This is when death gets iffy.
One thing for a tree to gussy up
in a sequined gown, dance

a New Orleans ragtime tune
clear into the reprieve of silence.
One thing for a tree to step out

of a wallflower green, ignore
a partner, and shake until it drops
redness. One thing for a tree

to do a striptease, shiny article
by shiny article, stand in a pile
of gold, stage lights glowing

on nakedness. Another thing for
a tree, shy in an old-world shawl,
to let one hanky float over

a Viennese waltz, inviting
the embrace of the other, while
the sky's silk curtain descends.

Stigmata

The nearly bare branch holds up a brown-paper
valentine, ragged at the edges like a five-year-
old's cutout for a first-grade teacher.

Each leaf bled like religious stigmata
from hands, veins vivid with a currency of
red drip-dripping onto the country roads.

Each tree luminous, bursting brightly
like the heart of Jesus into flames,
sharing love before the world freezes.

Embroidery Thread

The gold clumped leaves
still hold on in midwinter,
glimmer, a thread on an

Episcopal altar pillow.
Cushion the cold bony
cathedral of trunks where

space abounds, demands
an inner uncluttering.
Bushes frayed with gold,

a knot on the underside
of the tapestry. The sun
brushes gold flecks across

woods. A veil of color
lifted by branches, held,
a corpse slowly carried

away. Leaves sweep, soar.
Monarch butterflies
go South to Mexico.

Blown like a candle flame
out, leave the black wicks
of solid winter trees.

LIKE THE MONARCHS

Like the monarchs returning, leaves
fly about my backyard when the wind
gushes, unsettling the maple. One leaf

is caught in the window like an insect
on display in an entomologist's box.
The other panes are empty as a

nought-and-cross grid. Scientists warn
of a world turning to fire as my yard
ignites itself in this season when

each tree strips down to bare bark
as if it can't stand the heat, wants
the sky's pool of blue to cool in.

STICKY

Tongues lick the sun
through the slow-snooze
of summer.

Trees bulge thickly,
laden beehives.
Gold oozes to

the earth; light
is caught on
the ground's flypaper.

TONIC

Who knew death could dazzle?
Trunks swirl in a gold liquid,
stir a rum-flavored drink from

a tropical isle. Who knew flecks would
spill into the air? The fairy dust
from a child's bedtime story.

Hard liquor, a tawny tonic
before an adult sleeps. A wand,
a vehicle for the young to

nod off. Is winter long enough
for us to slumber, sleep off
the spell of a floating autumn?

WITH APOLOGIES TO THE TREE

With apologies to the tree
that scribbled the sky
with lines of branches,

dropped notes
to the ground each fall,

was pulled the length
of a highway by a truck,
a pencil stacked in a box,

for giving me this
white leaflet of space
I now chop up with words.

Unwanted

Not friendly, these decapitated
heads: quarter-moon smiles,
the flicker of internal flames
a kind of mad chattering.

We pick up full melons
at the end of October,
hack them mostly toothless
to gnaw on the dark.

Already trees have thrown
down the treat of leaves,
but this is a trick: a face in
relief on a shimmering coin.

Martian features grimace,
buy freedom from a night
of extraterrestrial visitors
who try to land on our yard.

Sugar Daddies

Drip maple sweet, trees,
sugar daddies like ones
bought for Halloween.

October tricks, treats:
the treat, cheap-trinket
foliage. The trick,

bare branches, empty
wire-mesh baskets.
Autumn years flash

memory then not,
fritter, crumple. Trunks
will lift arms into

snow's filmy petticoat,
await the next layer.
Who could blame a tree

for being a sugar daddy,
throwing all loot away
just to be noticed?

Green Card

I wish the momentum of leaves
falling, crumbling, becoming dirt
could make me be part
of the earth too, get rooted.

Instead, their flight is like
the paper work of immigration,
whirling about, not landing me
here, not making me feel at home.

I tumble above the terrain,
skitter about, don't quite belong.
My green card doesn't turn brown
but keeps the perpetual sheen of my country.

METAPHOR HUNTING

The leaf on my windshield wiper might be
nature's parking ticket to tell me I'm in
the wrong place. Or it could be a fallen star

telling me the view up will be uncrowded,
particularly after the foliage burns, clears
the sky of debris. Or, a sequin on the arc

of a barrette, the wiper holds strands of hair,
the silvery wisps of rain. Or it could be just
a maple reminding me I was not just blown

in here by a semitropical island gust,
like a piece torn from a crumbling brown
map, but have ancestors who followed it

to Canada. Somewhere in the family tree
are those who knew the sweet sap a trunk
renders and what the sun can slowly yield.

The Sun's Clothes

I think of the tree's de-leafing
as the sun taking off its clothes.

True, the branches want to wash
the year right out of their hair,

bend into the sky's deep pool
to rinse themselves clean. True,

the trunks will stand naked
behind the modest sheets of snow.

What's to be done when a world
strips bare? My tracks in winter's

wrinkled linen are like buttonholes
opened, reveal earth's contours, swells.

Acknowledgments

The Country and Abroad: "Summer's Widow," "Moccasin," "Change,"
    "In Hock," "Falling"
Litchfield County Times: "With Apologies to the Tree"
A New Ulster: "Tulips in January," "White Light," "Winter Landscape,"
    "Mercy"
Poetry Salzburg Review: "Simply the Fourth," "Cruel Enough," "Ripe"
Seek It Anthology on Sleep: "Wrought Iron Bed"
Stand: "Snowfall," "Cornfield"

The following poems appeared in chapbooks funded by the Bermuda Arts
Council.

The Sun in Three Countries: "Sun Gold Tomato"
Maiden Voyage: "Star Map" "Green Card," "White Wash"
Hurricane Season: "Summer White," "Livid," "Summer's Beggar"

*Cover artwork, Vintage Star Map (originally printed in Edinburgh, Scotland,
1942); cover and interior book design and photographic treatment of the cover art
by Diane Kistner; Legacy Serif text with Foglihten titling*

About FutureCycle Press

FutureCycle Press is dedicated to publishing lasting English-language poetry books, chapbooks, and anthologies in both print-on-demand and ebook formats. Founded in 2007 by long-time independent editor/publishers and partners Diane Kistner and Robert S. King, the press incorporated as a nonprofit in 2012. A number of our editors are distinguished poets and writers in their own right, and we have been actively involved in the small press movement going back to the early seventies.

The FutureCycle Poetry Book Prize and honorarium is awarded annually for the best full-length volume of poetry we publish in a calendar year. Introduced in 2013, our Good Works projects are anthologies devoted to issues of universal significance, with all proceeds donated to a related worthy cause. Our Selected Poems series highlights contemporary poets with a substantial body of work to their credit; with this series we strive to resurrect work that has had limited distribution and is now out of print.

We are dedicated to giving all of the authors we publish the care their work deserves, making our catalog of titles the most diverse and distinguished it can be, and paying forward any earnings to fund more great books.

We've learned a few things about independent publishing over the years. We've also evolved a unique, resilient publishing model that allows us to focus mainly on vetting and preserving for posterity the most books of exceptional quality without becoming overwhelmed with bookkeeping and mailing, fundraising activities, or taxing editorial and production "bubbles." To find out more about what we are doing, come see us at www.futurecycle.org.

THE FUTURECYCLE POETRY BOOK PRIZE

All full-length volumes of poetry published by FutureCycle Press in a given calendar year are considered for the annual FutureCycle Poetry Book Prize. This allows us to consider each submission on its own merits, outside of the context of a contest. Too, the judges see the finished book, which will have benefitted from the beautiful book design and strong editorial gloss we are famous for.

The book ranked the best in judging is announced as the prize-winner in the subsequent year. There is no fixed monetary award; instead, the winning poet receives an honorarium of 20% of the total net royalties from all poetry books and chapbooks the press sold online in the year the winning book was published. The winner is also accorded the honor of being on the panel of judges for the next year's competition; all judges receive copies of all contending books to keep for their personal library.